The Poetry

of

Windwalker

by Dale Musser

Table of Contents

Poems Listed by Topic

Love and Erotic

Mystical

Dreams

Poems in the "Dreams" section are poems that have been written about actual dreams I have had, while on the surface they may not seem to make a lot of sense, if you read deeper there are lots of interesting goodies in them.

Nature

Miscellaneous

About Poetry

FORWARD

THE POETRY OF WINDWALKER is a collection of poems written by Dale C. Musser using the penname of Windwalker. Some of these poems originally appeared online in a poetry forum in the early 1990's using the penname of "Thal" a name that Mr. Musser used before becoming aware of the poet Ian Thal, in order to prevent any confusion Mr. Musser began using the name Windwalker to publish his poetry and changed the pen name on his previously published works.

The original spark for Dale to write poetry came in the 1960's after reading the works of John Updike, there he found delight in the everyday subject matter that Updike used for his works. During a brief period in the late 1960's Dale produced several poems many of these were lost when he relocated several time over the years but a few survived and are included in this book. There is a broad spectrum of topics represented, from sheer poetic nonsense, events and observations of daily life as well as erotic and romantic poetry. This is not a book intended for children and is fully intended for adult readers.

Poem 101
Dream Love
by Windwalker

Last night I dreamed I held you in my arms.
We lay, your bare back pressing against my chest,
your head resting on my left arm.
My right arm draped around your waist,
my hand lay on the mattress beneath your breast.
Reposed in silence, we did not speak,
listening to the sounds of insects
singing through our open window.
A warm night breeze crossed your body,
carrying your scent to me.
I inhaled… and my heart quickened.
The rise and fall of your body,
with every breath delighted me.
A slow rhythm, like gentle waves swelling on a shore.
I marveled at your life, the miracle that is you.
You drew deep breath and I knew that you were awake,
staring out the window with me, at the stars.
I could feel your heart beat.
I willed my own to match its tempo.
For a moment our pulses matched,
you sighed and pulled closer to me as if
you sensed the oneness of that instance.
The warm softness of your skin was intoxicating.
I wished to press my lips to it, but the tranquility
at that place was so strong I could not move.
My feelings for you grew immeasurably.
We laid there like two shells nested one within the other.
I did not wish this dream to end,
this dream which has never been a reality,
and never will be.
I would gladly have slept forever,
resting in an eternal embrace, with you.
I fear I shall never dream that dream again,
but I shall be haunted by it,
knowing that I shall never hold or touch you,
tormented by the realization

that we shall never be more than we are now,
and never again be what we once were.
But as on this one occasion
sleep did in it kindness bring you to me,
I can but hope that soon it shall bring you to me again,
and that perhaps in time,
when death shall take me into that final sleep,
I might dream this dream into eternity.

~~~

Poem 102
Whose Thoughts
by Windwalker

Fluted thoughts sound across the ridges of the mind,
an ethereal vision results, a reality yet to be produced.
Sounds on beams of light, focused attentions to
the elements of life in Promethean ways.
Transfixed in the multifaceted aspects of these abstractions,
amazed by the complexity of my thoughts.
Is there another inside me who molds these introspections together?
I do not believe myself the author of their magnificence.
I feel a thief if I profess them my own.
Why have they shaped themselves here?
I have no regard for their topics.
They seem to appear from nowhere.
Mysteries unraveled, questions answered that I have not asked,
As if an unseen mystic stands at my side and whispers in my ear.
The enlightenment of these apparitions frightens me.
Interrogations could unravel me if I am asked to elucidate these
morsels.
I recognize their truths but my comprehension goes no further.
In my grasp I hold recognizable pieces of an indiscernible puzzle.
Shall I sit in silence with these gems?
Do I share them with the world,
only to appear the fool that I am
when asked for further explanations?
Or in my ignorance have I failed to see that
they are in fact only insignificant drivel
manufactured by my overactive psyche.

~~~

Poem 103
Look Down
by Windwalker

I don't get it!
"Look down around your knees,
mental midgets in disguise."
Is this some sort of cosmic joke?
Where was I when the act began?
Intellectual delusions, a masturbation of ideas
brought to completion by thoughts produced
in less than perspicuity.
Come now! Surely one can do better than this!
Six oranges at a dollar a dozen,
can be calculated even "IF" the computer is down!
Where is the deterrent in incarceration
when all the entitlements of labor are
substituted for penalization?
Has logic been replaced by the untenable?
At what point did I take that left turn in life
resulting in my relocation in the Twilight Zone?
And who the HELL keeps stealing one of my
socks out of every pair?

~~~

Poem 104
Black Bird Knows
by Windwalker

Black bird knows,
he picks in the hole in the walk.
Turning his head to the side to
peer deep inside with his yellow eye,
with agile hops he performs a mystical dance,
black feathers shinning,
his shrill call erasing the silence.
Eve's son and daughter,
conjured by a feathered prince,
join in the dance.
Around and around the hole they race
drawing ever nearer.
Then in silence, drop to their knees

3

and probe the opening.
Their short, stubby fingers
seek the night prince's treasure.
But even with dexterous digits
they cannot retrieve the French fry.

~~~

This poem describes an event I observed in 1973. I was at a small side walk café and noticed a black bird hopping around a small hole in the side walk. At times it would peck in the hole, trying to get some object. Eventually it began calling and two small children noticed its antics and ran to where the bird was. The bird flew to a nearby tree, while the children played around the hole, eventually looking in the hole and then probing it with their fingers. Curious as to what was in the hole that so captivated the bird and the children I walked over to see a single French fry wedged at its bottom, just out of their reach.

Poem 105
The Ballad of Toad
by Windwalker

Hark now and listen to this tale of woe
that calls to us from the earth.
Of beasties creeping in the night
and ladies in distress.
The story of a lowly lad
and of the maiden Bess.
Young Toad was what they called him,
none ever knew his name.
His parents were unknown stock,
as was from whence he came.
At night he slept in stables
in piles of sweet mown hay,
scraps he stole from the king's tables
he worked odd jobs at day.
He loved the king's young daughter,
a fair and lovely lass,
he'd wait on street corners,
each day to see her pass.
She did not note his shadow
nor glance upon his face;

he was a no-name peasant
who she must keep in place.
Now there lived upon the mountains
a horrid scaly beast.
It dined on rats and vermin
in bloody frenzied feasts.
But it longed for bigger morsels,
its appetite to fill,
and ventured to the village
late at night to seek a kill.
One day in famined hunger
it wandered into town,
in startled fright and horror
the people ran around.
In rage it scoured the village
it hungered in the street.
It came around a corner
the princess Bess to meet.
Confronted by its horror
she fought her very best,
the monster was much stronger
and stole her to its nest.
The king called forth his
army to rescue his dear child,
the soldiers balked in terror
of this beast so strong and wild.
Young Toad was white with sorrow
and fear for the fair Bess,
he volunteered his service
to go with the king's best.
The first wave of soldiers,
the beast killed in frenzied lust.
From bones he ate their marrow,
their blood dripping in the dust.
The second charge got further,
led by a noble knight.
Their lances tore the dragon
before it turned to fight.
With claws and teeth it battled,
knights and horses torn to shreds.

It stomped upon their bodies
and crushed their gallant heads.

Then archers launched their volleys,
their arrows stinging bees,
they bounced off the serpents hide
and fell around his knees.
The king then moaned in sorrow
for only one remained,
the humble peasant Toad
in garments torn and stained.
The king took his fine armor
and gave it to the lad,
to save his only daughter
he'd give up all he had.
But Toad was small of frame,
the armor did not fit,
instead he took a sword
and strapped it to his hip.
He found the beast distracted,
as it crunched on a knight's arm,
Toad looked on in horror,
had the princess come to harm?
His eyes searched in the dim light
his sight sought to find her dress
he needed confirmation
that life still breathed in Bess.
'Twas then he heard her sobbing
from 'neath a wooded hedge,
he tried to creep in closer
as to the king he pledged.
He crept into the haven
the fair young Bess had found
he stared at her in wonder
as she lay weeping on the ground.
He took her hand for comfort
and knelt to kiss her skin,
instead he kissed his thumb,
lest he commit a sin.
To press his lips on flesh so fair
by one so low as he

would be a foul act
a thing that must not be.
Poor Toad
so enamored by her sight
he had forgot the dragon,
he had forgot the fight.
A darkness loomed above him,
a foul breath he felt,
he quickly turned to find
the dragon now o'er him knelt.
Now Dragons have one weakness,
a soft spot known to few,
a place between their chin and throat
a small square inch or two.
Young Toad thrust out in terror,
he had no mark in mind,
but God grants luck and courage
to those with love in mind.
And so Toad's blade found weakness
and entered a deep vein,
blood gushed forth upon them
a hot and acid rain.
The beast let out a mighty roar
it staggered left and right
it trashed in dying anger
still looking for a fight.
In guarded stance Toad stood there
the princess to protect.
This time he would not falter
nor would the princess he neglects.
With one last breath and furry
the beast burst forth in strife
it crashed into young Toad
and then gave up its life.
Poor Toad was not so solid
nor as the monster strong.
His broken body lay there
he would not live too long.
The king rushed 'cross the clearing
and took Bess in his arms.

In dazed shock and horror
Bess did not see Toads harm.
But then with his light fading
Bess turned to see Toad's place,
a tear rolled down her cheek
and fell and touched his face.
His lips then formed a smile
and from this earth he passed.
The love he'd freely given
had been received at last.

~~~

Poem 106
Like a Sweet Wine
by Windwalker

Like a sweet wine, you linger,
a taste on my lips and tongue,
an intoxicating vintage to be savored.
You are an essence that abides,
coiled deep within the recesses of my mind.
A memory that begs to be re-freshened,
but never loses its bouquet.
I remember the blush upon your cheeks,
the fullness of your lips,
like plump, lush grapes.
The feasting of their sweetness,
how you fed me kisses with zeal,
how I could not be filled.
The fine, salty, beads of perspiration
between your breasts,
how I relished tasting them.
That hungry look in your eyes,
like a lioness preparing to take its prey.
I remember too your own musky perfume,
a maddening fragrance that filled my nose and mouth,
a scent that lingered on my skin for days.
Even now it echoes in my mind.
Like an addict I seek again your splendors,
to relish once more your feminine softness.
I wish to be with you to feast again and again

upon your nectars, a drunken fool,
lost inside your charms and in your heart.

~~~

Poem 107
He Was a Patchwork Quilt
by Windwalker

He was a patchwork quilt,
a tapestry in progress.
Formed out of scraps of life's fabric.
Sewn together by many hands.
When he came into her hands,
he was a work barely begun.
His pattern only hinted at vaguest images.
With tenderness she cared for him,
repaired loose stitches,
replaced old patches, worn and abused,
with brightly colored patches of love.
She arranged each piece with great care.
Always vigilant for areas of neglect and
in need of attention.
As she worked she wrapped herself in him,
and was warmed by his embrace.
His existence was secure in her care.
Each day more was added to his substance,
she snuggled deeper in his comfort.
Neither realized she had daily sewn
her own fabric, irrevocably, into his pattern
until at last they were one.

~~~

This poem was written without using words ending in "ing" or the words "the" or "that".

Poem 108
Standing in a Hall of Mirrors
by Windwalker

Standing in a hall of mirrors,
alone in a crowd of one.
Right and left faces,
peering at each other with the same dull eyes.

Mimics one and all,
mouthing silently my words.
Reality loses itself in the insane laughter of a woman.
I seek cracks in the floor trying to find exit.
Staring eyes of doppelgangers haunt me,
each seeking to take my place.
Certainty is absorbed by soulless reflections.
I am face to face with my back, there is no return.
Wet, invisible paint covers my body
a giant worm squirms inside my skin.
I glance in futility at the reflections around me,
hoping to see discomfort on their faces.
Their eyes mock me with possessing expectations.
Time and time again I rudely block my passage,
waiting patiently and unmoving if I stop.
I am relentless.
Despair is expelled by relief;
I view the empty frame and outside passage.
A pane of clear glass stops my egress.
I peer through just in time to see me leave.

~~~

Poem 109
Do Not Mourn Me in my Passing
by Windwalker

Do not mourn me in my passing
for I have grown weary of this path.
I have not traveled all that long,
but I have traveled very fast.
Life has treated me with kindness,
it has treated me with pain,
it has bestowed on me rich blessings
and it has taken them in vain.
It gave me friends in moments
when I could not walk alone.
It has left me in great sorrow
when forever they were gone.
It gave me love for others
that I've never felt returned,
in my heart it's placed an aching
that still within me burns.

I have seen great joy in a sunrise,
watched the waves upon the shore,
I've seen children building castles,
that don't exist there anymore.
I have listened to the birds,
as they sing sweetly in the trees.
I have smelled the fragrant perfumes
of the flowers on the breeze.
I have watched in awesome wonder
the eclipsing of the sun.
I have also viewed in horror
the evils men have done.
I witnessed the miracle of birth,
the first taking of a breath.
I have seen children in great fevers,
and seem them starve to death.
I have walked in many countries,
shaken many foreign hands.
I have dined with kings and princes,
and eaten with homeless from a can.
I have heard the singing voices
of the finest in the land,
I have witnessed great performances
by the greatest of the bands.
I have won awards and honors,
appeared on radio and TV.
While these things appeal to others
they have little charm for me.
I have shared things with the famous,
and the not so famous too.
I have done so many things,
and there are still many things to do.
But I no longer wish this life,
for it has grown much too complex,
and though there are many things remaining,
it's death that I seek next.
And I have also grown lonely,
and I'm longing to go home.
To see once more before me
those old faces that I've known.

So do not mourn my passing
when my time has finally come.
Do not try to stay its coming
when my race is nearly done.
For I will not leave in sorrow
nor will I leave in pain.
I leave in fullest knowledge
that we all shall meet again.

~~~

Poem 110
Full Length Mirror
by Windwalker

You hide behind a full-length mirror,
there you wait in silence for the crowd to leave.
A controversy of your attendance, why you stay?
All significant conversations are avoided.
In this room you feed on bits of muteness,
like Alice when she dined on magic mushrooms,
you too hope to shrink in size.
In your reticence you believe you are invisible.
Like a specter you drift through the throng.
You hope to avoid any touch
that might alert others to your contiguity.
Anonymity is your resolution,
like the dodo you wish to be extinct.
You're the prisoner of social grace,
awkward ugly duckling in your mind,
you do not realize you are a swan.
You mistake the awe you are held in
for displeasure and dislike.
Wit and charms surround you
and astound all in your presence.
Your grace and aloofness speaks to them
you attract them in like moths to light.
You are a goddess in their sight,
you are the one they adore,
the one they have come to see,
yet you hide yourself from these.

At your words all go into silence,
the sound of your voice sings to them;
in your words are truth and wisdom.
You are afraid, honest and wise.
You are Athena, Diana, and Helen of Troy,
you are all that is good and kind.
You are woman noble and true.
Step out from behind your mirror,
lift your face to sun for all to see.
Be that which you are, and be proud.

~~~

Poem 111
Whizzing in the Roses
by Windwalker

Whizzing in the roses,
a pure delight.
The thought of her nose there,
sniffing them tonight.

~~~

I haven't a clue what made me write this. (yes I know I'm a very naughty boy)

Poem 112
Nude Boy Laughing
by Windwalker

They hate to see the nude boy laughing,
mocking them in their filthy coverings.
In three-piece suits of adulterated wool,
and polyester nightmares draped to cover their souls.
The nude boy laughs at their coated shame,
as they try to hide their aberrant souls.
Their attempted distraction with gaudy garments
fails to hide their disease.
He dances, his beauty and grace manifested before them.
His purity blinds them.
They shield their eyes with dark tinted lenses.
He sings with a voice rich and clear,
it cracks their souls.
Tears wash the dirt and make-up from their faces,
lines of life chiseled despair are revealed there.

With love and sympathy it touches their hearts,
they are healed.
Sores and pain-ridden joints become whole once more.
In jubilation they divest themselves of their teguments.
With gratitude and lightness they join in his parade.
They seek out others to set free.
Their burdens left lying in the street.

~~~

Poem 113
I Read Your Words
by Windwalker

I read your words and want to puke!
Rhyming words with no thoughts or feelings.
Synonyms and Antonyms failing to coalesce into
any worthwhile meanings.
Where are your fire, passion, and anger?
Heart felt emotions that speak to our souls.
Where is that unbridled lust that
yearns to burst forth from your loins,
and makes us gasp with arousal?
Is there no passion in you,
ripping at you essence,
screaming to be heard?
Release its cries!
Do not stifle their flurry!
Do the words not burn within you?
Do not temper them with beauty.
Sugar coating them like candies to
sicken us with their sweetness,
but expel them with all the force,
brutality, lust, love and anger you feel,
only then will you be a poet!

~~~

Poem 114
Bargain Shopper
by Windwalker

Toilet paper, fifty cents off on a pack of six,
across town, not at this store.
A dollar for gas, round trip, a real bargain,

14

must go back to return the lamp which does
not match the decor.
Shucks, Wilson's next door has toilet tissue
for less I repeat the trip to return the rest.
It is good I'm so frugal and very wise.
On a six pack of Charmin's I saved fifty five.
Oh! By the way dear, the car needs gas!

~~~

Poem 115
Cyclops Eye
by Windwalker

There was color before TV,
but the Cyclops bleached it from the earth,
and stored it in his eye.
Children of the box, blind to
scents and touch of life around,
caught up in a colored world
of virtual reality.
No cotton candy on the merry-go-'round.
No sound of birds, or buzz of bees.
The kiss of the sun falls not on these.
TV popcorn in a microwave bag.
TV dinners on a plastic tray.
Ocean foam replaced by a Jacuzzi whirl.
Riding bicycles in the room,
going nowhere.
Cyber vision, cyber dates,
cyber sex, safe and sterile.
Cyber babies, just you wait.
No needs for cars, buses or planes.
The Cyclops takes you there with just a stare.
Within his hypnotic gaze all future is lost
as reality comes in second place.

~~~

Poem 116
Poets
by Windwalker

We are cripples all,
here to display our maladies,

to seek sympathy and understanding.
To be healed by an unknown messiah.
We bare our deepest wounds,
festering in the meat of our souls.
Scars of fear that incapacitate us displayed,
timidly, sensitive to the slightest diagnosis.
From beneath emotional rags,
we reveal our concealed leprous state,
we stretch forth arms to beg for mercy.
We feel with nerves rubbed raw by abrasions.
Our words inscribed like pox marks
bear witness to our sufferings,
they shunned by most who see them.
Yet we reveal them seeking compassion.
We view the world through
stained or tinted glasses
depending on our dispositions,
a kaleidoscopic and fragmented view.
We strive to share the visions of
love we see with our astigmatic eyes,
affection oft rejected by those beheld,
seeking beauty in imperfections.
Our sufferings are a contagion
we share them like contaminated food
seeking comfort in numbers,
solace in mutual anguish.
We are pariahs in society,
a bane of all mankind,
an unwanted conscience.
We are the poets!

~~~

Poem 117
A Place of Colored Sticks
by Windwalker

In a place of colored sticks, red, black and white, he found me.
"You must finish this," the eight-foot guardian said,
standing before me with a countenance of old dark leather.
Devoid emotions on a chiseled face of brown stone,
onyx eyes peering into the deepest regions of my soul.

~~~

Fatigue begged me to rest in a field of dull gray ash,
my naked body lying, a discarded empty husk, by the rocks.
A wind played rasping, out of key, melodies passing though my
bones.
The lizard's skeleton by my side mocked my resistance.
With faded energies I reached for its bone tail.

~~

At the touch a magic born,
and from the dust the flesh reformed.
The reptile scurried from my grasp
and hurried to the dry and brittle brush.
In its tracks colors returned to the land.
In passing green sprouts of life emerged on every shrub.

~~

Under the vigilance of the giant,
the Mother Earth fed and restored me.
"It is time for you to change your name,"
the watcher said, and disappeared.

~~

Poem 118
In Truth and Beauty
by Windwalker

In truth and beauty she was the Light
that illumined me in my darkest hour.
Caressed by the softness of her words,
which stroked my temples,
soothing my cares.
Her concerns touched my heart and healed its wounds.
My soul was lifted,
burdens lighten and I felt loved.
I wanted then to lay my head upon her breast,
to feel her body's warmth.
The touch of her fingers in my hair.
To have her rock me gently,
to rest for a moment in time and space.
We were not lovers then.
She became the mother and I the child.
Her wisdom covered me with loving tenderness.
I received it like rich nourishment from her.

17

It fed me and made me stronger.
It gave me courage to carry on.
There, in that moment I wept in softness,
and the grief within me died.
It was not what I had sought.
It was what I needed.

~~~

Poem 119
Bridal Wave
by Windwalker

Surfing on the crest of a Bridal Wave,
unrolling before her splendor.
Multicolored, scented drops splashing on her feet.
Her sun kissed skin draped in white foam.
Her hair, golden rays of sunlight screened by a wisp of cloud.
Riding the wave she'd always dreamed of,
never looking to see if she is headed for the beach,
or the rocks.

~~~

Poem 120
The Wreath Bearer
by Windwalker

There's a rock in my shoe that causes me to limp.
It's been there since the day before,
it will probably be there the day after.
I tolerate its presence, it is a reminder,
the voice of the of the wreath bearer
whispering in my ear,
"Remember thou art mortal."

~~~

Poem 121
The Fabric of my Mind
by Windwalker

Your memory clings to the fabric of my mind,
like a fragrance marks a room.
An essence deeply embedded in the upholstery,
paint, and woodwork of the recess in which I live.

I find you embedded in the core of my being.
Stuck in that place where thoughts take form in the soft clay
before hardening in the fires of reality.
Your imprint is everywhere; it shapes my thoughts,
influences my desires, and directs my future.
I dare not contemplated the effect of inhaling you so deeply.
You are an exotic redolence, irresistible, a narcotic.
I savor the tastes, consumed with desire to partake more deeply.
Repeatedly I availed myself of you, each time accessing more,
fueling the flames that forge my destiny.
I cannot escape the truth of your presence in my life.
You have become my center, the core around which I revolve.
No desire in me is separated from your existence;
I seek no escape, no release.
Captivity in your charms seems as a reward.
I am as the blood in your veins
coursing to the beat of your heart.
There to wander till the end to time.
I exist only as a thought now.
Alive only when you call in into remembrance,
fearing that one day I shall be forgotten
and shall cease to be.

~~~

Poem 122
No Significance to this Poem
by Windwalker

There is no significance to this poem,
just a bunch senseless verbiage,
like the words of a critic
critiquing what he cannot do,
or what he envies.
The work of a mind lost in self repose,
like the buzzing of a damaged hive of bees.
One sage expressed that poetry need not have meaning,
a truth informally demonstrated here.
Words, like scents floating around,
some incense rising to lofty heights,
others verbal flatulence assaulting our perceptions.
Pretenses all, the concoctions our fantasy prone minds
seeking escape from reality.

Gilded Gift-wrapped packages of emotions
rejected by a proper society in any other form.
Lost in a Sargasso of floating locution,
entangled, weighted down and nearly drowning,
we struggle to find meaning,
longing to find understanding,
and bare our souls.
A midst sharks and other predatory
denizens of deep feelings,
we bleed, again and again, hoping to gain healing
by the letting of our inner self.

~~~

Poem 123
Besides Herself and Inside Out
by Windwalker

Besides herself and inside out,
with bags, and cans,
and cardboard bits.
She wanders the street
with a shopping cart and
preaches philosophy to the wind.
Her roof is a freeway
her house has no walls.
She listens to voice
that speak day and night.
She's someone's mother
but they don't know her fate.
She does not remember their birth
or their face
or the name of her mate.
And people who see her,
give her a brief glance,
few of them wonder
and even less care,
for she is of the nameless,
a downtrodden cast,
the invisible ones that all of us pass.

~~~

Poem 124
Vanquished Footprints
by Windwalker

Puffs of wind vanquish footprints from the dust,
predecessors to monolithic variations of lemon tears,
a washing of mahogany clay.
Blinded by dark lightening,
deafened by silent thunder.
Soulless beings seeking salvation,
viewing their reflections on sandstone walls.
Empty bellies fed with starvation's fruit.
Toil in repose, defeat in victory.
In death and desperation man returns to the fetal nest.

~~~

Poem 125
Open Window
by Windwalker

Your open window sets forth
yeasty scents of fresh baked bread.
Hungers carried on a humid breeze.
Through the opening I gaze at your fruity jams,
marmalades with tart sweetness.
Memories creating cravings to indulge.
You taste the jelly from your fingers,
your eyes glued to mine,
working your soft, pink, tongue,
retrieving sticky sweet and sour drops.
You tease me with an invitation to the feast,
knowing full well this meal is for one.

~~~

Poem 126
On Marbled Plain
by Windwalker

On marbled plain of spinach leaves,
with apple cores and rinds,
beneath an upset cotton cake,
and under painted slime,
there is a reason for this poem

21

a lifetime full of sin,
a broken record meant to play
the silent sounds within.
Its wonders bore us all to death
and beat us into shape.
So let me stop this stupid verse.
I am a hairless ape!

~~~

Poem 127
Freeway Fools
by Windwalker

Freeway fools who know no rules,
ought to be in auto pools.
Diving like there are no others,
while we all curse their unwed mothers.
Racing, pacing, changing lanes.
One can see they have no brains.
Passing across that solid line,
driving slow when you're behind.
Looking in their rear view mirror
while their make-up they do smear.
Tailgating at 75,
if you break who'd be alive?
Drinking from mysterious cans
beverages which all states, drivers ban.
With disregard they work the radio knob,
or blow the horn and act a snob.
Kissing and fondling on the Interstate,
is hardly a safe or romantic date.
After all, Really! Can't they wait?
Think twice you fool, do you want this mate?
Alas as we travel these roads in life,
we travel not in safety, but in strife.
So if you want to reach your destination
try to drive with consideration.

~~~

Poem 128
He Lies, Peaceful in Repose
by Windwalker

He lies, peaceful in repose, without a breath,
and stares in silence at a mirrored ceiling.
Beyond the looking glass statues move,
frozen in a panic escapade,
rescue in suspended animation.
A score of ballerinas dance before his eyes,
choreography in shimmering light.
Time has stopped.
Dark coldness becomes brightness and warmth
as the drum beat slows and fades into eternal night.

~~~

*I wrote this poem after hearing a description of breaking through ice
and drowning by a person who had been revived after such an event.*

Poem 129
Will You Come and Talk
by Windwalker

Will you come and talk to me?
Will you share with me your secrets,
all your secrets dark and deep?
Will you tell me what you're thinking;
tell when and where you've been?
Will you tell me of your passions,
will tell me of your sins?
Will you reveal your deep perversions,
which make you shiver with delight?
Will you tell me of your lusty thoughts,
on dark and lonely nights?
Will you tell me of your lovers,
and how they made you swoon?
Will you tell me of the rhythms,
in your soul that you dance to?
Come tell me all your lusts and hungers,
tell me of your needs and your desires.
Tell that you want me,
tell me where, and tell me how.

23

Come tell me of your weakness
and I will make of you a slave,
and I will show you passions,
that feed your hungered lust.
I will play with you in your perversions
on kinky lusty nights,
and we will dance in the sweet music
in which your soul delights.
Come talk to me... Share with me your secrets!
Come and do not be afraid!
For if you tell me all your secrets, I will tell you mine.

~~~

Poem 130
The Sea I Love, the Sea I Hate
by Windwalker

The sea I love, the sea I hate,
the sea that gave me what I ate.
The misery that you gave to me
I now give back to thee.

~~~

This poem was composed during a violent reaction to scallops, which I happen to be allergic to. By accident I consumed some of these morsels on a seafood platter. Moments later while driving along the Virginia coast I began getting violent stomach cramps. Realizing I was about to be ill, I pulled over and ran down to the water. On the way to the water the first two lines of this poem popped into my mind. I reached the ocean and relieved myself of the agonizing contents in my stomach as the final two lines popped in my head. Years later I wrote this poem in the log book on a local tour boat. I was surprised the following year when on a return trip I found my poem on a plaque mounted appropriately on the ships rail. This is a true story.

Poem 131
Naked on Life's Highway
by Windwalker

Naked I rest on life's highway.
A sleeper on that fine line that
divides one lane from another.

About me freight haulers of the night
transport their cargos oblivious of my presence.
Obnoxious exhaust vapors assault my nostrils;
their passing creates breezes that chill my flesh.
Like a deer I am blinded by the glare of their lights.
Unable to drift to the right or to the left,
I am forced to walk that confined band,
endlessly moving deeper into ignorance.
Before and behind me stretches infinity,
there is no variance in either direction.
The trucks are my only company,
there for brief seconds before they pass,
unaware of my existence and soon
gone never returning.
I ponder their destinations.
Are their ends to their journeys?
Do they too travel ceaselessly,
like me on my narrow path,
never to find a destination.
Perhaps there is no more to life than this.
Each of us seeks to escape our course
we hunger for a goal where none exist.
Perhaps there is significance only in the journey.
Perchance it is how we run our race that determines our fate.
Or it may be that we all are lost forever.
Each to wander aimlessly on our webs
in deep reflections of a reality that does not exist.

~~~

Poem 132
Safe as a Relationship
by Windwalker

Safe as a relationship
where my shrunken head is
a toy for a sharp clawed cat.
A Queen's pawn.
A sacrificed self.
Unwanted love.
I march into battle,
with no look back,
to see the face of the one I love.

Naked, I run in a field or thorns,
in pursuit of an elusive butterfly.
Sweat and tear salts infiltrate my wounds.
Bile is my only refreshment.
With whips I scourge myself.
I drive the nails into my hands and feet
I raise myself up on a cross,
I die for no one!
I am the court fool.
The jester royal.
The dreamer of dreams.
The reaper of nightmares.
I am despair, agony and woe.
I am realization lost.
I am alone.

~~~

Poem 133
Water Skiing Behind a Killer Whale
by Windwalker

Water skiing behind a harpooned killer whale,
on an oil black, mirror flat sea ,
towed serpentine, twixt islands of debris.
Sounds of the cry of gulls,
and the water swish as the skis,
break the stillness.
Archeologists dig on a sacred beach,
oblivious to my arrival.
Elated by their find,
'Future Ruins' of space and time.
A foot falls on pieces of mosaic floor,
rubble disappears to be transposed
to new sights and sound.
"The show is ready to begin,"
a voice from nowhere cries.
The tickets almost sold,
I find myself in line.
To press a thumb upon the spot
that signifies my place.

I find myself hung up in space
A rocket launches before my eyes,
a huge and terrible thing.
The people o-o-h! and a-w-h-h! in glee.
An encore they demand.
On second run it's not the same,
a funeral scene instead.
A tyrant borne in a casket.
Hitler in coffin with lipstick on his face.
Nazi guards insist we view this monkey in a case.
People squirm and try to flee,
at gunpoint forced to view mockery.
The actor makes a face,
laughers are beaten in disgrace.
And so act II does end,
the audience grumbles, files out,
while hooded monks stand on the stage
and discuss depravity and foolish waste.
"What does this mean," I in panic cry,
just when the lights go out.
Act III begins, it looks like II,
it seems worn out, it is not new.
Behind a curtain on the stage
the monk peers out at me.
With frantic effort I cross the play
to boos and hisses from the fans.
We flee, through props of bygone plays,
I hurry to keep pace.
For many levels we go down,
below the crowd above.
We pass beyond their view,
and further still their knowledge.
In the basement of the soul
we finally pause midst sympathetic company.
The conscious of society, the awakeners of the mind,
the searchers of the truth.

~~~

Poem 134
To Their Ancient Family Homes
by Windwalker

To their ancient family homes,
the Gathers bid them come.
There, books, open wide,
records and memories bared.
No words of protest uttered at their revelations.
No errors found in their accounts.
Above the blue fabric of the sky
stained deep purple by spilled wine.
In its midst a cold white orb blazed.
The hope of all humanity.
Refuge and escape for all,
save twelve times twelve thousand.
"Why have we been left behind?"
Went up their cry.
From deep within an open box
a Stranger brought forth beans.
"What are these?" he queried.
"They're SEEDS," They in unison replied.
Wisdom stared them in the face,
the explanation came.
"And so, you have been CHOSEN to abide.
To others they are BEANS."
Marvels fill the sky, they descend like rainbows,
to touch the favored few. Powers of re-creation,
restoration fill their hearts and minds.
They are the Elected, The Healers of the Earth.
The Chosen few. The Restorers of Life!

~~~

Poem 135
How Jung Are You
by Windwalker

How Jung are you? she asked.
I ponder her interrogation.
Did she desire to know if my
self-inflicted tortures come out of past abuse?
Do I create my difficulties out of some need?

28

Had she seen in me that conflict which
provokes me to substitute gross sensuality
for prurient spirituality?
Had my addiction been exposed?
Am I suspected of being an instrument in that vast
breeding ground of psychic epidemics?
A fool proclaiming follies first and loudest?
Or am I the brilliant teacher providing the
nutrients on which growing minds feed?
Has she seen that because I love so much
I must truly love myself,
regardless of my protestations?
How Jung am I?
As Jung as she wants me to be!

~~~

Poem 136
Frozen Pirouette
by Windwalker

Caught in a frozen pirouette,
dancing at 65 miles per hour.
You capture the eye
with your smooth ebony frame.
Your image in a vertical pose,
reclined on a cardboard mattress,
a sensual delight of asexual pleasure.
I seek your fixed, blind, gaze,
my existence is naught to you.
A ballerina on a mobile stage,
accompanied by a symphony of horns.
You dance midst the musicians,
deaf to their out-of-key calliope.
Transfixed I follow for miles,
until destiny turns me from your path.
As I watch you pass from sight,
I wonder, is this your first dance,
or your last?

~~~

The inspiration for this poem came after following a truck on the
freeway with a mannequin on the back. The thought crossed my mind,

was it a new mannequin on its way to a store for display, or an old mannequin that was being taken out of service.

Poem 137
Toilet Seats for Golden Behinds
by Windwalker

Silver toilet seats for golden behinds,
What silly thoughts in people's minds.
Perfumed water in the toilet bowl,
a seat that has a radio and plays rock and roll.
Visions of fairies in the sky,
fluffy clouds go floating by
but on the street, on ragged stones,
our feet grind up our broken bones.
We live with mysteries all around
while the sages with logic can't be found.
Thousands of dollars for a pair of breasts,
on which the eye had best not rest.
Criminals all get three meals a day,
and sleep on beds for which we pay.
Yet the vet stands begging on the streets,
and digs in the trash for the meals he eats.
And kids in schools are taught by fools,
who play by convoluted rules.
To learn to march to common beat
is the only curriculum they must meet.
The preacher tells us to love one another,
while he picks the pockets of his brothers.
And Love has become a four-letter word
that is seldom practiced but too often heard.
Each night we sleep with our elected mates,
to which we are welded by uncommon traits.
And we smile in the daylight and weep in the night,
to keep others from seeing the truth of our plight.
So I ask you now, as one who is caught in this race,
HOW THE HELL DO I GET OUT OF THIS PLACE?

~~~

Poem 138
Medieval Past
by Windwalker

The knight knelt in the quigley marsh,
upon a peaty mass,
he fumbled with his armor,
to try and scratch his itching ass.
While on the path, and cross the moor,
with heads besotted by yeasty ale,
a rag tied band of humans trod,
over rocky hill and dale.
In castle keep, atop the crag,
the king sat on his throne.
He yearned for a hemorrhoidal cream –
The queen could hear him moan.
Below on streets with honking geese
and pigs in mire and murk,
the soldiers marched, in knee deep mud,
behind them people smirked.

A princess dressed in silk and lace,
dreamed a handsome prince,
and 'neath her skirt her hand did flirt
to touch the secret place.
And so this story, as is told,
in truth reflects those days of old,
and were this bard in that same past
this poem would be my very last.

~~~

Poem 139
She Knew Him by Heart
by Windwalker

She knew him by heart,
his life a melody that played in her soul.
A melancholy refrain accompanied
by the simpatico resonance of her existence.
A duet, a simple theme,
repeated in verse.
At times in dissonance,

31

though never really out of key,
but mostly in sweet harmony.
He was a tune that cycled in her life.
Once she heard it, never forgotten.
It played endlessly in her mind.
She danced to his music,
soared on his crescendos,
and wept in the darker somber movements.
She was young when she first heard him.
Over the years the tune remained the same,
new instruments were added to
the already rich sound of his composition.
She swooned to it adding her gentleness,
contributed to writing the off takes to his song.
Now she sits in silence,
his tune no longer in her ears,
her feet no longer waltzing to his beat.
But in her mind the tune still plays,
because from the very beginning
she knew him by heart.

~~~

Poem 140
Gypsy Moth
by Windwalker

Gypsy Moth dances in a flicker of a candle flame
a beauty for all to see.
Her ballet on air in beams of light
that captured the soul of me.
Gypsy Moth dances in a flicker of a candle flame,
if I watch, it will be I who gets burned.
For one so surely earthbound as I,
would find my attentions spurned.

~~~

Poem 141
Internet Love
by Windwalker

Nondescript keys click quietly before a silent screen,
emotionless letters,
coalescing themselves to passions and desires.

Through twisted passages,
spiraling conduits of cybernetic process,
they find their way to distant places,
there to activate their Full-blown lusts.

~~~

Bits of nothing and of one.
Excited by finger touch alone,
transporting such intense motions.

~~~

From out of the vacuumed darkness
they pour live and strong,
reinforcing and uplifting the intended one.

~~~

Poem 142
Old Dinosaur
by Windwalker

Old dinosaur sits in his lair,
remnant of a bygone era.
A mind frozen in Paleolithic attitude,
life in frozen fossils,
empty foods for starved needs.
Feeble eyes caress lines of faded text
on yellowed paper of generations past.
Cyclops's words and revelations…ignored.
Avoidance trying to still Time's hands.
Adam and Eves multicolored sons and daughter,
a spear in his side.
Sight and sound of joint labors….
an abomination.
He cannot fathom their impartiality.
In his sheltered grotto he gnaws on
gristled bones of ignorance and hatred.
Truth and knowledge are his enemy.
Reality a hideous dream
from which he cannot awake.

In still darkness he sits alone,
illumined only by light of an oil lamp
fed from a fuel of his own decay...
until he is at last burned away.

~~~

This piece was written without utilization of the word "the"

Poem 143
Satin Sheets
by Windwalker

Your life in adoration
on satin sheets of pain.
Your blood red lips in mourning
in smiles all so vain.
You move beneath the horrors,
of quaking quivering flesh,
to find you body flattened,
into the mattress pressed.
And in the morning stillness,
when the deed is long since done,
you find the bills upon the chest
and give them to the sun.

~~~

Poem 144
A Truth Half Told
by Windwalker

She licks the chicken from her fingers,
capturing my eye with her lips
Time turns into a slow liquid
I gaze in wonder …,
transfixed by her tender mouth.
My breath quickens,
a fire igniting in my chest.
I contemplate the taste of her lips.
She sucks upon her thumb,
her tongue, swirling round it
in the softness of her mouth.

Rooted in my thoughts for a moment,
I too taste her thumb,
as if my lips surround it.
She stops and looks at me,
"What?..," she says,
having taken notice to my stare.
"Do I have something on my mouth."
The illusion shatters.....I reply,
"You did, but it's gone now."
I am amused by my answer,
a truth half told.....,
for indeed my thought had briefly
been upon her lips.

~~~

Poem 145
Duet
by Windwalker

Passion blush on cheeks,
the fevered warmth of her body
and the longing in her eyes
were a melody in my soul.
A symphony played within
we were compelled to dance to its melody.
Primal rhythms, overrode the beats of our hearts.
We became marionettes to its motions.
Captured and held fast in our gazes,
we danced ever more exigent steps.
Obsessed with the intimacy of the ballet,
each movement a new delight.
Ecstasy in Arcadian motion.
Illumined by lunar glow,
we languished in temporal ecstasy
at that moment when time stopped
and for the beat of a heart we were one.

~~~

Poem 146
Sister Morphine
by Windwalker

Sister Morphine danced in the street.
Cute and saucy with seductive grace,
she spun her magic spell.
Enchanted by her splendor.
I followed in her wake.
Her sweet simplistic needs,
adoration and attention,
called to me like the song of sirens.
Intellectual curiosity fueled my hunger,
personal cares forgotten in her presence.
Addicted by her charms
and in her sweet embrace,
all agonies from my brain erased.
Late at night she came to me,
in safe and lonely rooms,
she my Beloved, I her Solomon.
She was the North Pole.
I the compass turned always to face her.
She infused me with her magnificence.
Her essence coursed throughout my veins.
I sought her warm kisses,
at her touch passions ascended,
cares and woes disappeared.
In fevered delights all self was lost in her.
In her absence I suffered pain and need.
In her presence all was color and light.
In her exit the darkest night.
Withdrawal agonies disfigured my brain.
My heart pleaded cessation in her departure.
My body sang most mournful songs.
My tortured mind cried for release.
I shivered as Emptiness ate at my soul.
Sister Morphine flirts and teases,
she dances in the streets.
People turn to see her beauty,
they admire her wit and charm,
they write her sweet refrains.

I too still marvel at her spirit,
but she no longer sees me there,
among the refuse at her feet
a discarded and forgotten shell.

~~~

This piece was deliberately written avoiding the use of words ending in "ing". This poem is not about drug addiction, Sister Morphine is a person, not a drug, but she is every bit as addictive as a narcotic. The effect on the men she seduces has all the appeal of the drug she is named for, and the pain and agonies experienced by her withdrawal are every bit as devastating.

Poem 147
Seekers of Truth
by Windwalker

Seekers of truth gathered in musty ruins.
Congregated to divine age-old mysteries,
confirmations sought for solitary dreams.
Is it truth they really seek?
Would they know it if it bit them in the ass?
Why do they contemplate their navels,
while humming out of key
to the beat of one hand clapping?
Can truth be found in a void?
Something from nothing?
Have they reached nirvana… alone?
What proofs do they seek for their revelations?
Do they accept them blindly,
faith contrary to all reason?
In their karmic revolutions have they discovered
an identity they can live with,
or have they finally discovered
each man makes his own path?

~~~

Poem 148
Why Don't You Face Me
by Windwalker

Why don't you face me when you say hello?
If you're glad to see me where are you eyes?

Has my countenance become so small I cannot be seen?
Have I become a deformed, ugly toad?
We meet in crowds and are instantly separated.
We do not speak to each other,
yet you thank me for our conversation.
Do you know that we have not spoken?
Do you care?
I voice questions,
your ears seem deaf to their sounds.
My words hanging motionless in the air,
an embarrassment to my sincerity.
Are there no topics for us to discuss?
Have we solved all the problems of mankind?
Do we not have common interests?
Have you no opinions to share?
I feel I'm an unwelcome guest at a party,
invited as a courtesy,
but not expected to attend.
I stand in hunger at this feast,
offered small morsels on a tray,
quickly removed before I can reach.
I thirst and see the wine flowing
but have no glass to drink it from.
Do you fear that if we speak
I will tell you I still love you?
Do you fear to hear my words,
or fear others may hear them?
Are you afraid of my emotions?
Or is it what's inside of you,
you fear to see?
And if you do what it could be?

~~~

Poem 149
Who Said Breathing is Free
by Windwalker

Decongestants so I can breathe,
Antihistamines to prevent a sneeze.
Asthma inhaler to stop a wheeze.
Who said breathing is free!

~~~

Poem 150
The Wife
by Windwalker

She dressed in a fashion
that was not quite her own.
Bore a name that belonged
to another.
She lived in a place
that was not quite a home,
wed a man who was
more like a brother.
She gave him three children,
and raised them quite well,
though she never felt
like their mother.
For deep in her heart
was a secret best kept
as she's lived in her
out of sync life.
For what she truly desired,
and too which she aspired
was to have been another
man's wife.

~~~

Poem 151
I Dare Not Look
by Windwalker

I dare not look into thine eyes,
whose magnetic orbs once gazed upon,
feed my soul with messages so strong
and deep my heart near bursts with joy.
I dare not look into thine eyes,
lest in my longing I convey
a truth that they might see....
A truth that could embarrass thee.
I dare not look into thine eyes,
for fear of all they tell,
though in truth I long with
all my heart within your eyes to dwell.

39

I dare not look into thine eyes,
for I a coward be,
I could not stand,
nor want to live
if rejection there I'd see.

~~~

Poem 152
Ode to the Commode
by Windwalker

Oh odoriferous throne,
in porcelain white,
on which all men are truly equal.
We salute thy majesty.
You see us at our worst,
take our misgivings
without complaint,
and listened to our lamentations.
You have absorbed our illness,
over indulgences, and
young men's emitted fantasy lusts,
never once voicing a complaint.
Oh, true, from time to time,
you get too full of our
offerings to digest it all
and need to be purged.
But for all that you must bear,
your unbiased nature is to be commended.
You have been a boon to all, rejected none.
So let now salute you!

~~~

Poem 153
I'd Like to Write a Poem Today
by Windwalker

I'd like to write
a poem today,
but not one muse
has to come to play.
Just to craft
a phrase or two,

or write a poem
for you -know-who.
But alas my mind
is in a rut,
I can't come up
with even smut.
To have no rhyming
thoughts of sex....
I fear to think
what might go next.

~~~

Poem 154
Mind If I Join You
by Windwalker

"Excuse me, do you mind if I join you,"
she said.
"I hate to eat alone!"
There she stood, tray in hand,
looking ever so like a vestal virgin
with offerings for some pagan deity.
A tight black dress
retaining most
delightful curves.
Of course I didn't mind,
I'd be a fool to reject
this morsel for the eye.
I must confess
I neglected my food
as I feasted on her beauty.
I found myself in avoidance
of being caught staring
at her delightful cleavage.
Her lips and eyes were things of beauty.
Her words rang in my ears,
reverberating like temple bells.
Was she flirting with me,
I wondered.
Dare I venture to further our acquaintance?

I mumbled garbled sounds,
an effort to communicate,
speaking my best Neanderthal.
How could she have been impressed?
My heart beat louder
than my voice.
And then …
her salad consumed,
she thanked me and left.
Perhaps all she really
had wanted was
company while dining.

~~~

Poem 155
I Wonder
by Windwalker

I wonder if knowing then, what I know now,
if I'd have dared to wait...knowing all too well
ramifications of times and space,
would I have waited to try and woo you,
knowing between us lay a score of years?
Would I have felt the risk worth taking,
surly the prize is great....
Or in more contemplative mind,
recognizing unfairness to thy youth and beauty,
given rise to such quandary, would I have
shrugged and walked away in pain and sorrow,
knowing there may never be another come my way.
I wonder....
And even now I wonder....
given chance that change could happen any day
or things go on forever as 'tis now, dare I love you?
For surly I could love you as I never have another,
knowing no more than I do,
but I wonder....
I wonder at the things I cannot give,
a child, the vigor's of my younger years.
One could argue to the shortness
of time span allotted to us,
but history shows the folly of this argument,

for no man know when comes his hour,
nor at what age he may be called.
but still I wonder.....
And if by heavens glorious blessings
all things should fall to place,
and if thy eyes fell solely on my face
and shone with love so bright that all in life
seem naught ...I wonder.
It seems at times I am God's pawn
and all this his game,
though none of this makes sense to me
I love you all the same...and still.....
I wonder!

~~~

Poem 156
Wooden Box
by Windwalker

Her heart she kept in a wooden box,
round her neck the key.
For those looking for love
she had nothing to give,
yet her affections she gave away free.
Men stood on her steps
to woo her at nights,
these she would never see.
But she kept deep in heart, in the wooden
box, the hope of a love to be.
Now how does one get to a heart,
in a wooden box,
in conditions such as these.
How does one show a lady
his love, when this very same love
the lady refuses to see.
How can one pick the lock,
or get to the key
if he is to show her that he....
is the one meant for her heart
who will never depart,
especially if that someone is me?

~~~

Poem 157
Sea Green Eyes
by Windwalker

I stare into your sea green eyes
that so quickly change to carry me
from sea, to sky, to forest,
and in me something stirs my heart
to beat a faster, stronger pace.
My eye is captured by your charm.
Every line and pore Gods work of art
painted on the canvas of your soul.
The finest hairs upon your arm...
I would touch each with gentlest caress,
it's thoughts like these that
urge my heart to faster beats.
Your face so near to mine,
your words spilling forth like wine
filling my ears until I am drunk with them.
I revel in their sounds,
seeking to drown myself in their elocution
Your breath touches on my face,
my heart loses pace, I am maddened.
I seek to press my mouth to yours,
to feed upon your lips,
to meet your tongue in its own place
and there embrace.
Closer still it seems you draw,
my breath near leaves me as I swim
in your aura. Waves and fingers
of ethereal delight dance on my skin
and mind, all seems brightness and heat.
There is a sweetness in the air,
brought on by bodies in such heat,
that moves men's minds beyond control
to passions sweeter still than those
so far known, and I would go there
if you please.
But still you linger,
moving me to such heights

until it seems that heaven
itself is moved by all I feel.
The earth rocks beneath my feet.
Your eyes staring intently into mine
fixing me in such a state
that mortal men like I
cannot contain such joy.
It seems my breath has matched you own
and now my heart led by yours.
And though no touch has thus far passed,
between us I do swear I can feel the pressure
of your breast upon my frame.
But deeper still movement stirs within my chest,
for you bring forth something in me that is best,
and so I pause, and wait your pace,
for 'tis not yet time, nor is our place.

~~~

Poem 158
Come
by Windwalker

Come, and gently lay thy head upon my chest
and let thy breath upon my flesh caress,
in sweetest tender touch thy love proclaim.
Come, let fall thy hair, and let it frame thy face enchanted.
A picture finer still than artists ere can produce,
let me feast with eyes alone upon thy beauty.
Come, touch your lips to mine, and let me drink that wine
that from thy lips flows, a sweet and passioned drink.
Flowing, flowing, yet never satisfies my thirst for more.
With arms about my neck and lips to mine be pressed
the wine let pour. The pumping of your heart feeds still
till I in ecstasy lost, near drown in bliss.
Come, let us dance in horizontal plane,
a dance of sweet refrain on varied steps
of rhythm beats, a long and raptured ballet.
Come, walk with me through life, hand in hand,
and stand with me on mountain peak, let us
see the glories of the land, and share with me this life.

Come, do not from me depart, for thou hast stolen my heart,
for if thou should go from me there is no dream
can ere remove the pain of solitude and grief.

~~~

Poem 159
It's Raining Here Today
by Windwalker

It's raining here today, drops beating on the roof so hard
it sounds like violent drummers out of control.
The roof protects my skin from their wetness,
but the pounding drops penetrate my soul,
leaving me with a sadness inside,
like a woeful face carved into my pumpkin like heart.
I wonder where you are, do you also hear the rain?
Does it wet your heart as well?
It seems sunshine is always in your heart,
lighting and warming others with its brightness.
I need that brightness.
I sit in the easy chair, staring out the window.
Watching the droplets run down the pane.
Somehow they have gotten past the glass and to my face
I can feel them running down my cheeks.
It is quite here, save for the beating of the rain,
quiet and empty.
I hear the ticking of the old wall clock,
counting off the minutes since I last saw you,
counting off years of my life.
Tic…a second gone…Toc…one more,
each lost into eternity, never to be seen again
never to be replaced. Somehow they do not matter,
only the moments together with you have meaning.
I look at the bed, still unmade,
the place where you laid next to me, cold now.
I cannot bring myself to lie there,
for the cold, only adds agony to the
warm memories of your presence.

Outside the water pools, forming small streams
that wash away the tracks of your leaving.
In the morning all evidence of your having been here
will be gone, save for the wetness left in my heart.

~~~

Poem 160
Palms Caress
by Windwalker

There is something delightful
about the way the cavity of my palm
conforms to the curves of your body.
Your blushing cheek
warm against my palm,
your breasts smooth
yielding as your nipple
teases my palm.
The firmness of your buttocks
as I caress them.
The warm, humid
cleft mound between your thighs
that seems perfectly molded
to its shape.
I must remember not to take
this palm for granted,
and remember also that in its caress
it too can be delighting.

~~~

Poem 161
The Key
by Windwalker

I found a key the other night
and held it in my hand so tight
blood from my fingers dripped,
to mix with salty tears upon my desk.
No ordinary key was this,
but one for which one chance
exists to open up a treasured chest.
One chance, and only one,
for which is best to wait,

lest to soon used, or too late,
may seal forever in ironed fate
that lock.
I cannot not guess nor ponder,
if or when, that day or time and place
may come, that from my secret hiding
place that key may be withdrawn
to test that lock.
I cannot dare to hope,
nay yet try to speculate,
if even then this key may work,
or if by fates decree this be a key
long since past its using.
But I shall hold it tight within my grasp
and if that day should come,
when at last I hold it to the light,
with prayerful thanks,
and in an opportune delight, shall
take my chance to try and excite that lock
into release, its prizes to reveal.
But till that day, this key I shall conceal.

~~~

Poem 162
Little Sheep
by Windwalker

Little sheep with cleft feet
that feed on barren plains.
Their bleating sounds, on winds
rebound, in hateful, loving rage.
Upon a stage a silent sage
recites his muted piece.
While on her knees a
harlot page gives homage to her liege.
And in the wake of frozen ships
as captains steer their course.
We see the schools of drying fish
cooked on the oily shores,
and wonder what they learned
in school that teachers did not see.

It seems to me you're out of reach
and yet you've touched me so.
But how my kiss became a slap
is one I'll never know.

~~~

Poem 163
Identity
by Windwalker

Am I not allowed to be who I am?
May I only be whom you choose?
If I am not what you think,
then I don't exist?
It is a choice to understand me.
To choose to see my shades of gray,
you have chosen not to see me as I am.
Must I be black or white,
one thing or the other,
can I be nothing between?
Love or indifference,
loyalty or betrayal,
I am, or I am not.
Either I fit into your mold
or I do not exist.
So easily dismissed.
The flavor of life becomes so bland
when "goodbyes" are easier
than dealing with reality.

~~~

Poem 164
Verbal Toys
by Windwalker

Words, verbal toys
tricks for our ear and eyes,
deceiving to believe we
understand other's thoughts and feelings.
Words, symbols carrying
multitudes of meanings
seldom received as they are given.

Lines, curved, and dots on paper,
or grunts, gasps and wheezes in sounds
arranged, and rearranged in patterns
meant to paint mental images and feelings
on the canvas of our souls.
Tiny fragments that can
create a peace, start a war,
thrill a heart or break a soul.

~~~

Poem 165
There is a Place
by Windwalker

There is a place where we could meet,
a place that none can see,
the light that shines within our eye's
or hear the softness of our words
as we our love could speak.
There is a place where we might meet
in warmth and solitude
and there our troths and pledges keep.
There within in my arms you'd softly sleep
and none would ever know.
But I do not love you thus.
Nor would I hide my love for you
in dark shadows, stealing passion
from your heart as if a thief.
Rather, would but that we boldly,
hand in hand,
walk in the light of day,
our love a monument for all to see.
With pride and fullest love felt joy
to walk by your side,
blessed by the sun,
that all may know the love that flows
so deep, may not be cast upon with
with lightness by a mortal man, or god.
But till that day when such may be,
I'll have to simply pass and nod.
Accepting the smile on your face,
passing words of pabulum taste

and pray that I my place can keep,
and that my dreams are not in vain.

~~~

Poem 166
Rejection
by Windwalker

I fear my words of love
have become scorpions and wasps.
Syllables and phrases that sting
your soul with reminders of love
you feel for another.
I am grieved.
Grieved I may not tell you of my love.
Grieved my love fills you with pains
in remembrance of another,
Grieved my love brings you no joy.
I am at a loss.
I dare not love you lest I give you pain.
I may only be a friend.
A friend on whom you may lean
A friend on whose shoulder you
may softly weep in moments
when your heart aches in memories of him.
And yet I cannot not bare to go,
to stray from your side.
I have lived so long with the stings
of the scorpions and wasps
my face no longer displays their pains.
I can live with the torment in my heart.
I can keep my words of love inside
and I will stay by you,
until I am replaced by one you love
and you have sent me away.

~~~

Poem 167
Sibelius Plays
by Windwalker

Sibelius plays,
instilling thoughts of you

that brush gentle on my mind.
A touch of a soft warm fur
on the bare flesh of my heart.
A bitter sweet refrain,
haunting my soul,
reminding me of my longing to be with you.
I hear laughter in the strings,
voices of muses humored at my desire.
They know my supplications.
I am teased with your beauty and light...
so fair, attracting me as a moth to a flame.
Sibelius plays,
I am immersed with you
in warm and scented waters.
Your fingers gently entwined with mine.
I am blessed at this transport.
Brought closer to you by a melody,
suspended with you in a moment of time.
A place created by sound.
Sibelius plays,
you become a swan,
swimming on still reflective waters of my soul.
I feel in you the sadness,
I grieve at your loss,
I seek to soothe your pain,
as you drift in the stillness.
Has Sibelius found your soul?
With Sibelius's sounds I found you
with his wondrous tones defined,
but when his music stops playing
you still are on my mind.

~~~

Poem 168
Thoughts Embrace
by Windwalker

Thoughts of you surround me
a warm, welcome embrace.
My heart is lightened.

In blue skies I see your face,
your voice is carried to me
in a bird's song.
You are a gentle fragrance on a breeze.
Sun rays warm my skin,
they remind me of your touch.
Nature speaks of you…
she smiles on her blessed child.
I am captivated by your existence.
Enamored with your wisdom.
Blessed by your communications.
I long for your presence
I find comfort in your memory.
Were it possible I would never part from you.
If permitted I would be at your side forever.
For in you I have found that which makes me whole.
All that is good, all that is best.
With you I am truly blessed.

~~~

Poem 169
Sweetly Now I Speak to Thee
by Windwalker

Sweetly now I speak to thee.
Gentle blessing that thou art,
with words of love,
which from my beating heart
have come to dwell upon my lips.
For fairer flower has not this earth adorned,
than thy fair bloom.
A flower so sweet and fair.
One I may not touch,
lest thy petals I might bruise.
Nor dare I tread too closely to thy root
for damage there I too might do.
Alas it seems that I am doomed to
gaze upon thy beauty from afar,
and pray that gentle breezes,
may on their back carry
thy sweet and fragrant scent to me.

From morn till dusk my eyes shall
dwell upon thy beauty,
and then in darkness,
in sweetest slumber,
dream thy petals brush upon my lips.

~~~

Poem 170
Whose Tune
by Windwalker

I listen to the music
and I think of her,
and wonder ...
who it is she dreams of
when she hears the music?

~~~

Poem 172
Nurse McGee
by Windwalker

"Poop and pee," says nurse Rachel McGee,
"Tell me about your poop and pee."
"But I'm here about my busted knee!"
"A busted knee!.. it's no interest to me!
Please tell me about your poop and pee!
Is it soft? Or is it hard?
Do you shit it by the yard?
Do you shit in little turds,
Or is it messy like that of birds?
Does it coil left, or coil right?
Is your stool loose or is it tight?
Can you see the corn you ate
and what about the smell of late?
Hurry answer, ain't this great?
And what about your urine stream?
Does it burn and make you scream?
Does it dribble on your shoes?
Does it leak out while you snooze?
Is it dark or is it light?
Do you go often in the night?

Please tell me about your poop and pee,"
begs depraved nurse Rachel McGee.
"But what about my busted knee?"
"First tell me about your poop and pee!"
"My poop is fine, I pee's all right.
Now fix my knee, that is my plight!"
A sigh escapes from nurse McGee,
"All right!… I'll tell the doctor of your dilemma,"
she exclaims.
"But if your stomach starts to bubble
and it begins to give you trouble,
if your excrement comes out double,
or if your pee is not all right,
please ask for me, Rachel McGee.
My specialty is poop and pee!"
~~~

Poem 173
Passions Heat
by Windwalker

You stare at me through lidded eyes,
glazed with passions heat,
speaking to me in primordial
sounds, of ancient powerful magic,
instilling such lust for flesh as
drives men mad.
A fever consumes my mortal flesh,
as your silky leg bends at knee, your foot
dragging seductively along the sheet
enticing my eyes to gaze upon
your wondrous treasures.
You immobilized me with
this magic spell you weave.
The blush upon your cheeks
your open lips begging me to feast.
Soft and sensuous curves
of neck and breasts,
and now I can no longer speak
for you have sucked
all breath from my being
with your beauty.

55

My hands and lips follow
where eye has been
molding, cupping, kneading,
kissing, nibbling, sucking ...
as a child at mother's breast.
Your arms surround my neck,
your hands stroking
my hair, and back, and sides.
We search each other
seeking out secret places to explore.
Until at last our pleading
souls sing to tunes of bodies
played in finest orchestration,
an overture of such proportion
that the universe explodes in
thunderous ovation.

~~~

Poem 174
Visit to a Muse
by Windwalker

I went to see my muse today,
held exiled deep in my soul's dungeon
where years ago I placed him for
pains he caused me.
It had not been easy placing him there,
yet his longings had been more than I could bear.
He still longs for your kiss,
A Kiss he has never known.
Kisses given to another who discarded
them on dark streets and in common houses
like a thief who cared little for their value.
He spoke of your sweet scented hair,
how he desired to feel your soft skin
touch upon his own.
To hold your hand,
to see a smile on your lips.
To share a sunset.
He spoke of holding you in his arms,
speaking to you softly as you doze
on a lazy afternoon,

things that never were,
things of which he still dreams.
It was not easy listening to him,
he still tortures my soul with his desires,
squeezing my heart with words
of his love for you,
…when I let him speak.
I had hoped perhaps to release him
so he might once again fill my heart
with core emotions and feelings.
To let me be human once again,
to love and feel loved,
thinking perhaps now time was right.
I had hoped!

~~~

(This poem has been written without using the word "the")

Poem 175
Come Thou Death
by Windwalker

Come thou death and with thy sweet embrace enfold me.
I hear your voice whisper "It is time…!"
I weary and wish no more to travel on this path.
Embrace me! Carry me forth into that eternal slumber
of dreamless sleep into eternity.
Come and do not tarry,
leave me no longer in despair.
Do not tease me with your quiet enticements,
I long for your sweet and lasting kiss.
There are no futures here for me!
No loves, no joys, no rewards.
Come take me from this misery.
Leave me not with sadistic disregard!
Do not joy in my grief and longings!
Come, delivery me from this life,
Carry me into eternal death,
Seal off my breath forever.
All that is life and hope are now denied me,
all that I seek now is in your coming.

57

The race is run and I have lost,
hopes and dreams have been destroyed.
All that is left is your embrace.

~~~

Poem 176
If Pain Were Love
by Windwalker

How blest would be if pain were love
and that which in my chest doth beat
were joy instead of grief.

~~~

Poem 177
To Be the Wind
by Windwalker

How I long to be the wind
that tousles with thy hair,
and brush upon thy cheek,
putting wind kissed blushes there.
Your scent I'd carry on my breeze
and waft it through the air.
I'd circle bout thy face and
lips caressing them with care.
Oh how I'd love to be the wind,
the air that you inhale.
I'd bring you mountain freshness
and scents of lilies from the vale.
Warm breezes in the evening
I'd wrap about thy frame,
and whisper in thy ear
your loveliest of names.
And when at night
your head upon a pillow rests,
I'd sing through pines a lullaby,
and whisper prayers that you be blessed.

~~~

Poem 178
Sadly He Sits
by Windwalker

Sadly he sits
absorbed in intellectual thought
trying to resolve his state.
Restitution of a life lost
in less than perfect pursuits,
seeking justification for behaviors
spent in mindless pleasures.
Can there be credit for absence,
can lessons learned too late replaced
prudent judgments?
Sadly he sits,
failing to realize his contemplations
squanders what remains of his time,
chasing regrets instead of accomplishments.

~~~

Poem 179
The Road
by Windwalker

Where are you going?
Starting here and ending there,
Standing still…
and yet,
being everywhere,
between,
at once.

~~~

Poem 180
Trees of Youth
by Windwalker

In my youth trees were magic,
a willow by a brook became
mountain caves one day
and castle havens yet another.
Long rope like branches
became whips to speed our horses,

two stumps that stood next to
an old log appeared as a stage coach,
pursued by bandits one day,
or a schooner chased by pirates, another.
At times stronger branches became arrows
other days we wove thinner ones into small baskets.
A cluster of maples at yard end
appeared a fort,
on other days
older trees carried us into outer space as we
placed ourselves conveniently in seat like branches.
In summer we fed heartily from two cherry trees
along a dirt lanes edge,
their juices running down our faces,
our hands and mouths sticky with sweetness.
In fall, when leaves fell,
we raked them into huge piles,
leaping and playing in them until
once again they covered all bare earth around.
Winters were solemn.
I did not like trees of winter.
It seemed they mock me with their bareness,
rejected me with their still silence.
They were as cold and remote as
winter itself, appearing
dark and dead in winters fading light.
But in spring,
as days grew longer,
trunks slowly became a bit greener,
buds thickened on limbs,
promises of friendship bloomed
growing to become another summer of adventures.

~~~

Poem 181
Meeting God
by Windwalker

My son died...
Eight and one half hours on this earth
and he died.

How do I tell you what I experienced?
What I saw...?
His still small, un-crying body
So white, so pale,
So perfect in appearance,
So still in the nurse's hands
as she placed him in a clear plastic box.
Of the concerned look on the doctor's face
The hushed words he spoke...
"Spine bifida
Heart displaced...
Lungs premature...
Surgery necessary...
Specialists...
Medical center...
Must transfer now...
Ambulance... police escort waiting..."
How can I tell you of the miracle?
Touching of that perfect mind,
that small,
still mind,
so full of brightness and peace,
beyond pain and suffering of the body.
I do not recall driving the distances
Between the hospital of his birth
and the medical center where a team
of highly skilled men and women
awaited his arrival.
The trip was filled with the vision of
THAT light,
THAT peace,
THAT wonderful peace,
at the touch of that small mind.
Some would say it was imagination,
wishful thinking on my part,
with death eminent my
desperate mind reached forth to grab some hope.
They do not know...
They cannot know...
I am not sure how I know,
But I do...

61

Hours later, after surgery,
Standing in a room
where three nurses stood,
never once taking their eyes
off the instruments and my child.
I stood looking at my son...
Reaching out once more to touch
that beautiful... perfect... mind;
So at peace, so warm in that beautiful light.
How can I tell you...?
In that moment I felt communication with the divine?
Tell you the choice was mine...!
This still small body...
So beautiful...
so at peace...
Tell you the choice was MINE...!
That his eyes could open...
that he could live on this earth,
that he would suffer the rest of his life...
but that his mother,
his mother who had never seen him,
could hold him in her arms...
that he would suffer,
with great pain,
with great disabilities...
suffer and live on this earth,
that he would never run and play
that he would need constant care...
but that he could be with us and we could love him.
That the choice was mine....!!!
How can I tell you...?
How can I tell you ...?
How can I tell you ...?
after seeing that light,
after seeing that peace,
after feeling that warmth...
that no amount of love,
or selfish desire,
could make me take him from
THAT peace,
THAT joy,

THAT warmth…
THAT love.
I walked from the room,
Still seeing THAT light…
Feeling THAT warmth…
and THAT love…
in his mind…
I knew I would never see my son again in this life
that for the rest of my time on this earth
I would live in pain and suffering…
I envy him in his peace,
in his warmth,
in the love that surrounds him.
It was not my imagination!
I am haunted by the memory,
torn by the desire to be there,
knowing all too well,
I do not belong there.
The sun was rising as I drove back to the other hospital,
back to take my wife,
just recovering from anesthesia,
in my arms and tell her
that our son had died!
How could I tell her I met God!

~~~

Poem 182
Without Love
by Windwalker

Without love we are like
trees without leaves,
cold barren…
unmoved.
Trees with leaves move gently in a breeze,
their branches reaching toward sky,
trying to caress heaven.
When we have love
we gently reach forth,
with warm caresses,
like summers breeze
touching all around us.

63

But when love is gone,
when it has left us,
like leaves of a tree in winter,
when we are left barren of its warmth,
we too become cold and unmoving,
hiding under gray skies awaiting for spring,
and loves return.

~~~

Poem 184
Resident Ghost
by Windwalker

It's 1:30 AM…
front door hinges squeak
followed by a sound
of footsteps on the stairs.
I hear them coming down the hall,
the smell of lilac perfume
mixed with cigarette smoke precede her
entrance to the room.
"NO SMOKING IN THE HOUSE!"
I tell her…
"You're welcome to stay,
but no smoking in the house."
The smell of smoke vanishes,
But the lilac scent lingers.
Every night I tell her,
every night it is the same.
Why can't I get this ghost to understand?

~~~

Note: This poem is based on real events. While this does not occur every night, it does occur many times a month, pretty much as described. While I do not believe in ghosts I am at a loss to otherwise explain this phenomenon.

Poem 185
I Don't Like Fall
by Windwalker

I don't like fall!
Trees losing their lovely shades of green,

slowly taking on colors
like a fever on a child's skin.
I don't like fall!
Everything turning brown,
leaves falling to the ground
a smell of decay dominating chilly air,
replacing the smell of flowers and life.
Fall is like death!
Trees bare,
dead like
cold.
Winds howl through sickly branches,
on earth leaves only rustle briefly
before turning into mulch.
Darkness descends
as birds and butterflies
migrate south in search of green life.
I really don't like fall!

~~~

POEM 186
Thanksgiving
by Windwalker

Turkey with skin all roasted and brown,
apple cider to wash it down.
Tatters and gravy
me oh my…
another slice of apple pie.
Cranberry sauce
and corn bread filling
my stomach is stuffed
but my mind is still willing.
Hot baked buns
and collard greens,
served right after
the ham and green beans.
Tomorrow I'll go shopping
to buy bigger blue jeans.

After this meal I must take a nap
while the dog and the cat
fight for a place on my lap.

~~~

Poem 187
Loves Question
by Windwalker

I do not wish to walk through life alone
my fate unshared... my joys unknown.
But rather that you walk with me
or I with you so as the case may be
to touch upon each little things
the joys togetherness can bring
To wade through life's refreshing streams
and share with you our every dream
these things I ask
and little more
Why is it to you I'm such a bore?

~~~

Poem 188
Mint Tea
by Windwalker

In an old orchard,
beneath apple trees
grew a bed of woolly mint.
Sweet fragrance,
a scented message,
carried on a summer breeze.
This mint,
in summers past,
a cooling fragrance
would entice until Grandfather,
with handfuls,
would place those fresh picked leaves
in boiled water...
then set aside to steep until
a greenish yellow hue appeared.
Then... with no particular measure
sugar added...

I would watch…
with greatest anticipation,
until this elixir poured into a metal can,
with a screwed on lid,
was placed in a cold spring by the barn.
There… nature its magic worked
while we some other chore attended
soon though we'd return.
Grandfather would take
down from a nail
an old metal cup
and pour in
that most wondrous beverage,
which I as a young man then,
and now old…
to this date have yet to find its better.
There was a look
on Granddad's face,
as he would sip that tea
and it would seem that for a moment
another time and place he'd be.
Now… years later,
when I in solemn celebration,
on summer eves my own
tea savor… leaves
taken from those very same stocks,
a look too passes ore my face,
as two men,
now…
from different times and place,
meet once more,
outside of time and space.

~~~

Poem 189
Mountain Romance
by Windwalker

There is a place,
in Rockies high,
where each year
waters burst forth

between two mountains…
Mother Nature's legs spread…
giving birth to Spring.
For nine long months
the mountain grew
her caps of snow
until at last…
the long sleep of winter over
she decorates her hill sides and valleys
with flowers,
blankets of green mosses,
ferns and trees.
The mountain peaks
are nature's breasts.
From them nourishment flows
feeding spring to
grow into summer…
to mature into fall
and then… when winters comes
…sleep!
In spring Heaven smiles
at the mountains beauty,
he seduces her with sunshine,
his seductive words
whispered on gentle breezes.
Charmed by his displays
the mountain yields to his advances
and the Heaven rains down on her
gently with his love.
As Spring grows into Summer,
Heaven's love grows
his passions stronger
he thrusts lightening into
the mountain with deafening
moans of thunder on his release.
All summer long he makes love
to the mountain,
until, his passions spent,
he begins to sleep.
The mountain,
Full wakened now by Heaven's

ardor seeks more.
She puts on her brightest colors.
She fills the air with dark and
musky fragrances into fall,
trying to regain Heaven's attention.
But Heaven, his energies spend
his passions becoming more subdued,
Slowly…
day by day,
pulls the clouds, like covers
over him until at last,
the light fading,
he goes to sleep.
Below, the mountains sigh,
Heaven's seed with-in her womb,
waits still.
Heaven in its sleep, discards its blankets
which fall to settle now on Mountain Peaks,
to cover her as she now sleeps,
Until once more,
another spring is born and
both awake once more
to see the other they adore.

~~~

Poem 190
Barefoot Boy
by Windwalker

Barefoot boy,
trying to stand tall in a forest glen,
what mysteries do your eyes see,
viewing the world with Pan's delight,
do you see the butterfly lifted gently by the breeze?
Is it you who makes the sounds in the trees?
Do the birds sing their songs just for you?
Barefoot boy, wading in a stream...
minnows nibbling at your toes
what secrets of this wild place do you know?
Do frogs and mice hide in your pockets?

Is it you the Owl asks about?
Barefoot, boy... was I once you?...
can you be me?

~~~

Poem 191
Mystic Baby
by Windwalker

My daughter sits upon my knee,
A baby who is but three.
"Tell me." I inquire,
a thought in her mind to inspire,
"What are you?"
"A doo-de-twerp," she replies
and so the table turns
and it is I who now must learn.
"A doo-de-twerp?
What's a doo-de-twerp?"
The mystic looks me in the eye
And with a sigh replies...
"A tree!"

~~~

Poem 192
Honey Kisses
by Windwalker

Come feed me honeyed kisses
let me inhale the sweetness
of your breath as
I gaze upon you beauty.
Let me place my hand in draw of your back...
pull you tight against me
let me trace your face
and lips with my tongue
feast upon them with delight.

Do not be coy with me
For now is not a time for teases,
passions heat has come upon us
like the rising and falling of the tides
carrying us on a journey
meant for the bold on love's adventure.

~~~

Poem 193
Coffee
by Windwalker

Coffee...
elixir mixer
sleep deprivation fixer,
breakfast drink of champions
the social drink
that helps you think!
The aroma...
eliminates sleep coma,
keeps you awake,
when your jobs at stake.
Drink it hot,
drink it cold,
drink it weak or
drink it bold.
Dry roasted,
freeze dried,
doesn't matter
it's still imbibed.
Put it in ice cream
or put it in cake
put it in anything
you'd care to make.
It comes as a liquor
an ice cream,
a cake,
or a candy.
Whatever the form
you will find it quite handy.
Have it with sugar,
cinnamon or cream

Starbucks will invent
something new
that you've ne'er before seen.
After all that you drank
please don't be surprised
if after you die,
they can't close your eyes.

~~~

Poem 196
The Shoe
by Windwalker

He was an old sole
in his early days
he'd been quite stiff
polished yet unyielding,
a real pain.
As time progressed
he grew softer and duller,
yielding to the pressures
of everyday life
becoming more causal,
less formal
until at last,
reflecting on his experiences,
he became quite holey.

~~~

Poem 197
Dogtooth Violets
by Windwalker

In spring,
on Middlecreek's
tree lined shores,
beneath huge Norwegian maples
the dogtooth violets grow.
These small flowers,
their yellow,
sun like brilliance show,
for two small weeks
and then they go.

It was these flowers I loved the best,
they signaled the coming of warm days,
put winter's cold to rest.
Their silent trumpet petals
seemed to put forth a note,
unheard to human ears,
to which nature would reply
with songs of birds by day and
choruses of peeper frogs by night.
Fifty and five years ago,
On Middlecreek's shores,
beneath those tall and stately maple trees,
I made a small stone lined bed and placed in it
some dogtooth violets.
Fifty years and five…!
In those years since
vines of poison ivy creeped
covering every tree
and rock with tendrils deep,
most threatening;
so it was with greatest care,
on my return,
I entered there.
Springs icy floods,
from every winter since,
have flowed across that glade,
carrying in their flow mighty
sheets of ice that smash into trees,
dragging across the earth
eroding away the shores.
I dared not hope…
but yet… there before me
a small stone frame that
bright within bloomed
a host of yellow shining
dogtooth violets.
A tear ran down my cheek,
I felt again the warmth
of the sun upon my skin,
I heard the birds begin to sing,

that night I heard the peepers' song,
and I was young again!

~~~

Poem 198
On Days of Darkness
by Windwalker

On days of darkness,
with noise in trees,
when bees with honey
shake their knees,
you'll see the stars
on a greasy sheet,
and listen to the sound
of a corpse's heartbeat.
You'll wonder if bats
ever fly a kite
as they sail on seas
without sunlight.
You'll eat the grass
on the barren hill,
and shoot the song
of the whippoorwill.
But you'll never sleep
on the concrete bed
while all these mysteries
still dance in your head.

~~~

Poem 201
Doubt
by Windwalker

With her eyes she pleaded
"Please love me!"
She leaned forward…
her lips parted.
He kissed her
a kiss that said
"I will love you forever!"
But she did not believe.

~~~

Poem 202
The Therapist's Chair
by Windwalker

For a brief moment
in time and space
the old brown chair
is the safest place.
In its cushioned comfort
one can speak their piece
reveal their secrets
and seek a release.
No fear of reprisal
no slaps in the face
here in this chair
one finds refuge and grace.
Here people listen
and ask "How is that so?"
with genuine interest
your thoughts want to know.
Their suggestions are tempered
to lead you to right
it's not their intent
to provoke you to fight.
Here no one tells you
that you are no good,
here you're respected,
here understood.
Though it's over so quickly
and one must return
leaving the chair for a world
where you're spurned,
you know there will be
safety and wisdom and care
when next week you return
to sit in the chair.

~~~

Poem 203
The Butterfly
by Windwalker

Greetings butterfly,
gliding on air in regal splendor,
your ornithoptic flight a magical display
mesmerizing every eye.
Your fairy flights delight us,
captivating us by your dance on air
flitting and gliding,
one flower to another
gracing their beauty with your own...
No one objects to your presence.
We are captivated by your splendor
too easily we forget your life
as a caterpillar,
stuffing yourself on green vegetation
until embarrassed by your gluttony
you hide in a cocoon where you
transforming yourself into a
ruler the air to sip on sweet nectar
midst sweet smelling flowers
as you sit on a pedaled throne.

~~~

Poem 206
Ruthie Ray
by Windwalker

Get out of the way
it's Ruthie Ray
pushing her shopping
cart on a sunny day.
Into that cart
the things that she tosses
these items are savings
and not financial losses.
Panty hose,
one dollar off.
If they are an odd color
you'd better not scoff.

This meat's two days old
it smells slightly tainted.
With the money she
saves she can have
house repainted.
The bargain shelf
is right in sight.
At this rate she
will be shopping
'til late in the night.
And when she gets home
just where will she park?
The garage is still full
from her last shopping lark.
The house has no hallways,
no table tops clear,
last week's bargains
are still stacked up by the mirror.
But it's not a problem
that she has to face,
as she is always out shopping
all over the place.

~~~

Poem 207
Earth Shadow
by Windwalker

At times,
earth its shadow
spreads across full moons gleaming
surface like dark rich honey
leaving in its wake
a bruised spectacle in night's sky.
In past,
men in horror watched
as the earth's finger puppet shadow show,
running like frightened children
with visions of
their moon to turn to blood
by some unseen galactic dragon.

Men and animals died in sacrifices
as the earth laughed in delight
at the frightened men trying to appease
some angry and unseen god.
Today no one pays attention!

~~~

Poem 208
Mystery Woman
by Windwalker

Mystery woman,
where do you come from?
what is your interest in an old man like me?
Your coyish charms
delight me.
I am drawn to you
like a moth to a flame.
is that your desire?
or are you, too, a pawn in this game?
Is it your mystery
I find so appealing?
Like quicksand I find
my endeavors to escape your
embrace only cause me to sink
deeper into your allure.
I do not succumb so easy
to feminine charms,
yet somehow
with relative ease
you captivate my attentions.
What motivates your actions,
and…
why do I so easily toss
normal cautions to the wind
neglecting my own dictates
for decorum and behavior?
My Muse finds you attractive
pricking my mind with sonnets
I dare not write.
He consults with Pan
on lascivious ideas

which they in concert whisper
in stereo into my ears
while cupid flutters his
wings before my face
distorting my visions of reality.
Tell me my lady,
are you some goddess,
commanding these demigods
to your service?
Am I some toy for the gods'
humor and entertainment?
Are you Aphrodite?

~~~

Poem 209
Ice Cream
by Windwalker

One double scoop
with sprinkles please
must eat it slow
lest my head freeze.
But if the sun is
boiling hot.
Eating slow
might melt the lot.
On days like this
it's such a quandary
perhaps I'll get an ice cream sundae.
Bananas, nuts with whipping cream,
cherry on top.... It's such a dream.
Or maybe a cup
with chocolate topping
once I start eating
there is no stopping.

~~~

Poem 210
Your Legs
by Windwalker

Your long legs thrill me,
like Jacobs ladder

they too reach to a place
of heavenly delights.
Your delicate ankles
so dainty,
a true delightful leading
to firm calves so shapely
teasing the eye with
their smooth lines.
Let one not forget the knee.
oh that lovely knee
which begs my hand to rest
upon it as you sit
at my side.
Just past the knee
those smooth inner thighs
with skin smooth as velvet,
how I love to caress them
with silken like finger touches
leading toward Eden's garden,
a place
where temptation
leads the serpent
to try to gain entrance.

~~~

Poem 212
Little Minx
by Windwalker

Oh what a little Minx you are,
sneaking stealth fully into my dreams
with your coyish charms.
Delightfully teasing me with
feather like touches,
arousing me in my sleep
only to impishly depart when I seek
to hold you in my arms.
How is it that you are able
to elude my touch and passion
while so thoroughly
penetrating my defenses?

I must confess it is not
your ministrations that I find objectionable,
for in fact they are most delightful.
But rather your own avoidance
of my desire to return the favor.
Perhaps, I too shall find
a way to penetrate your dreams
leaving you in passions heat
while I… in satyr folly
delight in your arousal and captivity.

~~~

Haikus
by Windwalker

Cute police woman.
Sixty nine speeding tickets.
Love needs re-fining.

~~~~~~~~~~~~~~~~~

Notice! In progress,
Out of mind experience.
Please do not disturb!

~~~~~~~~~~~~~~~~~

The pain of love lost,
is often more painful than
death of a loved one.

~~~~~~~~~~~~~~~~~

Royal sex capers,
monarchy in disarray.
Love needs refining.

~~~~~~~~~~~~~~~~~

Haiku! Haiku! (sniff)
I'm sorry. Excuse me please.
I have got a cold.

~~~~~~~~~~~~~~~~~

Marriage and asylums,
both require your commitment
and insanity.

~~~~~~~~~~~~~~~~~

Spring buds produce leaves,
that wave softly in the breeze.
Songs of birds in love.

~~~~~~~~~~~~~~~~~

Nudist colony,
a place where naked people
air their differences.

ABOUT THE AUTHOR

WINDWALKER is the pen name used by Dale Musser for his poetry, a name he received after going on a vision quest in 1998 with the aid of a Native American shaman. He was born in 1944 in the small rural community of Kantz, Pennsylvania, where his family owned and operated a general store. Behind his home flowed Middlecreek, an area that served to inspire much of Dale's poetry.

From 1967 to 2012 he was employed as a structural and piping designer in the marine and offshore industry, the cogeneration power industry and in hard rock metal mining. His work at three shipyards and assignments with several engineering and naval architectural firms during his career in Virginia, Texas and Maine took him to such places as London, U.K., Abu Dhabi, U.A.E., Scotland and Mexico. During this time, he was responsible for the design of nuclear aircraft carrier and submarine reactor compartments for the U.S. Navy and the structural designs of numerous offshore semisubmersible oil rigs, tanker ships, supply boats and other vessels and equipment used in the offshore industry. After the death of his wife in 1999, Mr. Musser changed careers and went to work in Arizona and Utah in the hard rock mining industry. He retired in fall of 2012 and currently resides in Mesa, Arizona; however, his plans for the near future involve a move to New Mexico.

Dale enjoys rock hunting and lapidary work, gourmet cooking, writing, poetry, art, music, religions and philosophies in small doses, astronomy and the sciences in general, hiking, camping, the outdoors, and the gifts that nature provides. Mr. Musser is a member of Mensa and avid reader, having lost count of all the books he has read after 3,000.

The greatest joy in his life is his daughter, Heather; affectionately they call each other "BUBBY."

Dale also enjoys writing science fiction and non-fiction works. His books are published under the name Dale C. Musser.

Contact Information:

Those wishing to write him may do so at dalemusser1944@yahoo.com. Though he attempts to answer all fan letters, the heavy volume of daily emails may prevent him from responding.